US Immigration Exam Study Guide in English and Albanian

Mike Swedenberg

All Rights Reserved
Study Guide
100 Questions and Answers for the US Immigration Test
in English and Albanian
A unique product, professionally developed and annotated
Updated 2023

The U.S. Citizenship Services (USCIS) administers a verbal test to all immigrants applying for citizenship. This study guide tutors Albanian speaking immigrants for the USCIS verbal citizenship test in English and Albanian. The questions have been selected from questions used on past exams by the USCIS.

Studying these questions does not guarantee obtaining citizenship to the United States.

Bi Lingual Languages available:
Spanish, English only, Polish, Albanian, French, Portuguese, Russian, Korean, Chinese, Vietnamese and Tagalog.
In Print and eBooks at Amazon.com
Plus an English / Spanish CD

DEDICATION

To all those working to become a United States Citizen

US Immigration Exam Study Guide in English and Albanian
All States

100 Sample Questions and Answers for the US Immigration Test
Updated January 2023

Twitter: @USAcitizenship

Study Guide
100 Sample Questions and Answers in English and Albanian
A unique product professionally developed and annotated
Translations from various sources including Google Translate.

Lists all current Senators, Congressmen, Governors State Capitols, Sample Written Sentences and Legal Advice from an Immigration attorney

Representatives are subject to change. It is your responsibility to confirm you Congressman, Senators and Governor.

The U.S. Citizenship Services (USCIS) administers a verbal test to all immigrants applying for citizenship. This study guide tutors Albanian speaking immigrants for the USCIS verbal and written citizenship test. The questions have been selected from questions used on past exams by the USCIS.

Studying these questions does not guarantee obtaining citizenship to the United States.

CONTENTS

ACKNOWLEDGMENTS

We gratefully acknowledge The U.S. Citizenship Services (USCIS)
for their cooperation.

Good luck on the test.

.

I pledge allegiance to the flag of the United States of America, and to the republic for which it stands, one nation under God, indivisible, with liberty and justice for all.

INTRODUCTION

The 100 sample questions and answers for the US Immigration test are listed below. The test is an oral exam in which the USCIS Officer will ask you up to 10 of the 100 questions. You must answer six out of ten questions correctly to pass the civics portion of the test.

On the naturalization test, some answers may change because of elections or appointments. As you study for the test, make sure that you know the most current members of Congress, Senate, Speaker of the House and Governor of your state and district.

This publication is the only study guide that provides this information and updates it throughout the year.

We also provide you with the Sample Written Questions which all applicants must know how to write in English.

What's New

For 2023 the Lists of Governors, Senators, Representatives (Also called Congressmen or Congresswomen), due to recent resignations and retirments. This information is included to help those who are new to this country and are not familiar with our system of Government and do not know how to find their Representative's names.

In response to many requests, we have included the contact information for the Senators and Congress members.

The legal advice from Immigration attorney Chris Kurczaba has been updated and expanded.

The Table of Contents has been expanded for ease of use.

A guide to U.S. State Postal Abbreviations has been added for the List of Senators

Advice
from the Immigration Law offices of
Kurczaba & Associates

6219 N Milwaukee Ave, Chicago, IL 60646

10661 S. Roberts Rd. #101– Palos Hills, IL

(773) 774-0000   www.KurczabaLegal.com

BECOMING A CITIZEN

The day of your interview, you will be asked to appear at a specific date and time at the

Immigration Office. For interviews in Chicago, our interview will take place at:

101 W. Ida B. Wells (formerly Congress Parkway), 3rd Floor

Chicago

Bring to the interview:

Interview notice

Passports – all your passports, current and expired

Permanent Resident Card (green card)

Driver's License/ ID

Income Tax Returns – bring your last 5 years of tax returns (may be asked)

Alimony/Child Support – (if required to pay) – bring proof of payment Check In:

Arrive 30 minutes before your scheduled interview

Check in with the receptionist (in Chicago - on the 3rd floor) – they will give you a number

You will be called by number

Interview:

When called, you will enter the officer's room, and:

Oath – swear that you will tell the truth.

Fingerprint /identification– the officer will take your photograph (using a digital camera) and ask you to place your left and right index finger on a little black box on their desk.

Administer the following test

1.TEST

Questions – 100 possible Questions – as listed in this book

You will be given 10 questions - 2 from each section,

You must have 6 correct. As soon as you have 6 correct – you pass and the question portion of the test ends.

Reading- you will be asked to read a question out loud to the officer (usually shown on an iPad)

Writing – you will be asked to write a sentence on the same iPad which is dictated to you. (in Chicago – this is often the answer to the question you just read)

2.APPLICATION

You will be asked questions from the Citizenship Application (form N400).

Biographical information

Name (your full name – first, middle last) as shown on your birth certificate

Any other names used – including your maiden (before marriage) name

Address, telephone,

Your marital status

Spouse's name, date of birth, date of marriage, immigration status (if out of status – you may state this, you may also state that you are applying for permanent residency for them). If your spouse is a US Citizen already, you may bring a copy of their Naturalization Certificate

Children – their names, dates of birth, locations of birth, current address (often city is sufficient)

Details on employment, residency

Travel History – when is the last time you left the United States? Sometimes officers will ask you have you left the United States since filing your N-400 application? OR Have you ever been outside of the United States for 180 days or longer? You may check your travel history on the Customs and Border Protection Website at: https://i94.cbp.dhs.gov/I94/#/home

> If you have been outside of the United States for longer than 180 days at any one time, be prepared to provide detailed information as to why you stayed outside of the country for so long. If for education reasons – provide proof of attending school, for job reasons – bring a letter from your employer, because of illness – bring proof of your seeking medical attention.
>
> > It is up to the Immigration Officer to determine whether your permanent place of residence is in

the United States, and there was good reason for you to have to remain outside of the country for > 6 months. Officers will look to the exact reasons for your staying longer outside the country.

In the past 5 years, you must have spent at least > ½ of that time in the United States. This means out of 1,825 days; you must have spent > 913 days in the United States. If you have not – you do not qualify for naturalization.

Did you ever serve in the military? When? What branch?

How you received permanent residency?

If you obtained permanent residency through a spouse – are you still married to that spouse? Bring proof with you including joint filed tax returns, bank account statements, insurance statements, proof of residency. If you are divorced – bring your divorce decree (issued by a court) and be ready to explain why you were divorced.

If you obtained permanent residency through an employer – be prepared to give information about your sponsoring employer, the name of the owner, address and telephone of the company, and the occupation you were sponsored in for permanent residency. The officer may also ask if you had experience in that occupation before being sponsored, and where you were working to gain that experience.

Your eligibility for citizenship – most asked questions – see later questions for a full listing.

Did you ever claim to be a US Citizen?

The immigration service has been adopting a strict approach to this question. If you have ever stated that you were a citizen, you can expect to be denied and the Immigration Service to start proceedings against you to lose your permanent residence.

Did you ever vote or register to vote in an American election?

Did you ever discriminate against anyone?

Did you ever lie to immigration/ use false documents?

Do you owe any taxes?

Did you ever file taxes as a nonresident (after receiving your permanent residency)?

Do you have a title of nobility?

Were you ever a member of the military?

If so – was it mandatory? When did you serve? What was your title/rank?

Do you have any weapons training?

If so – what kind of weapons?

Are you a member of a terrorist or socialist organization?

If a male, did you live in the US between ages 18-26? Did you register for Selective Service?

Be prepared to provide proof of the registration which you can obtain by checking the Selective Service Administration at https://www.sss.gov/Home/Verification

Citizenship Issues

Are you ready to take the oath of allegiance?

Did you read and understand the oath? (copy in this book)

If the law requires, are you ready to sign up to the military and defend the United States?

If the law requires, are you ready to assist the government in a civilian capacity in a time of national emergency?

OATH

You will be asked if you are ready to take the Oath of Citizenship. You should be familiar with what the oath says, but do not have to memorize it. The oath generally says that you will be loyal to the United States and defend this country.

I hereby declare, on oath, that I absolutely and entirely renounce and abjure all allegiance and fidelity to any foreign prince, potentate, state, or sovereignty, of whom or which I have heretofore been a subject or citizen; that I will support and defend the Constitution and laws of the

United States of America against all enemies, foreign and domestic; that I will bear true faith and allegiance to the same; that I will bear arms on behalf of the United States when required by the law; that I will perform noncombatant service in the Armed Forces of the United States when required by the law; that I will perform work of national importance under civilian direction when required by the law; and that I take this obligation freely, without any mental reservation or purpose of evasion; so help me God."

TEST

1. 10 Questions (6 correct)

2. Read a Question Out Loud

3. Write a Sentence

Three Tests for Citizenship

Most applicants for citizenship or naturalization as it is called, are subject to THREE different "tests" when applying. It is important that an individual understand that in applying for Citizenship their entire immigration history is being reviewed and an Immigration

Officer is making a determination not only over whether an applicant passes a test, but moreover, is reviewing the applicant's entire immigration history.

The Citizenship process should be looked upon as a complex, detailed demanding process, not just the completion of a form and passing of a simple civics test. This is not a process that should be taken lightly.

Often persons get "free" help with benevolent charities completing applications during large scale meetings. However, an applicant can face severe consequences including the loss of their permanent residency and even removal from the United States if certain matters come to the attention of an Immigration Officer reviewing your application.

First and foremost are persons who have ever been arrested, detained, or even stopped by a Police Officer.   These individuals should ensure they seek the assistance of an attorney to review their criminal record before proceeding with the filing of an application for Citizenship.

Each Applicant for Citizenship undergoes three tests:

1. Test of Civics/History/Government, Reading & Writing

a. Civics/history test of 10 questions chosen out of a possible 100

b. Reading – applicants will be asked to read out loud a sample sentence from a fixed set of possible sentences

c. Writing – applicants will be asked to write a sentence dictated by an Immigration Officer.

2. Ability to Communicate in English

a. The Immigration Officer will review your application with you. Traditionally, this takes place after you pass your test. This portion can be difficult for those that do not speak English well.

b. The Immigration Officer will speak to you in English to determine if you generally can communicate.

3. Eligibility –a review of an Applicant's personal history

a. The Immigration Officer will review your entire immigration file and determine if you have the proper character to become a citizen. The Officer will literally have before them your entire immigration history including every form and piece of paper that you submitted to the Immigration Service. This includes your applications for immigration benefits before permanent residency.

i. The Officer will review how you obtained your green card or permanent residency.

1. If you received your permanent residency through marriage to a US Citizen, then the Immigration Officer will ask questions about your marriage. The Officer can question whether the marriage was legitimate.

2. If you received your permanent residency through a family member – the Immigration Officer will review your original application to make sure there were no improprieties when you applied.

3. If you received your permanent residency through an employer – the Immigration Officer can ask you questions about the employer and the employment relationship.

ii. The Officer will review your criminal background – checking if you were ever arrested/detained/stopped by a Police Officer at home or abroad.

1. For the Immigration Service- to be stopped, arrested, or detained means precisely that – any time a Police agency would take your fingerprints

a. Regardless of the eventual outcome of the case – or what you think it means to be arrested – you will be expected to admit to all times that you were arrested/stopped or detained by a Police agency.

i. Sometimes applicants believe that an arrest means serving time in jail. But the Immigration Service has a much broader interpretation – including anytime that a Police agency would take your fingerprints and record the information.

ii. The Immigration Service obtains criminal background information on individuals primarily from the FBI. The FBI retains this information forever, regardless of expungements, or local agencies clearing of a criminal history.

AMERICAN GOVERNMENT

Qeveria Amerikane

A: Principles of American Democracy

A: Parimet e Demokracise Americane

1. What is the supreme law of the land?

> The Constitution

1. Cili eshte ligji me suprem (kryesor) I vendit?

Kushtetuta

2. What does the Constitution do?

> Sets up the government
>
> Defines the government
>
> Protects basic rights of Americans

2. C'fare roli luan Kushtetuta?

> Vendos qeverine
>
> Perkufizon qeverine
>
> Mbron te drejtat baze te nenshtetaseve Amerikan

3. The idea of self-government is in the first three words of the

Constitution. What are these words?

We the People

3. Koncepti I vete-qeverisjes qendron ne tre fjalet e para te

Kushtetutes. Cilat jane keto tre fjale?

We the People – Ne Njerezit

4. What is an amendment?

A change to the Constitution.

An addition to the Constitution.

4. C'fare eshte nje amendament?

Nje ndryshim (ne Kushtetute) - permiresim

Nje shtim (ne Kushtetute) - permiresim

5. What do we call the first ten amendments to the Constitution?

The Bill of Rights

5. C'fare quhen dhjete amendamentet e para te Kushtetutes?

Te drejtat e njeriut

6. What is one right or freedom from the First Amendment? (You

need to know one answer)

Speech

Religion

Assembly

Press

Petition the government

6. Emerto nje te drejte ose liri nga Amendamenti I Pare*

Liria e fjales

Liria e fese

Liria e mbledhjes

Liria per shtyp

E drejta per peticion ndaj qeverise

7. How many amendments does the Constitution have?

Twenty-seven (27)

7. Sa amendamente ka Kushtetuta?

Njezet e shtate (27)

8. What did the Declaration of Independence do?

Announced our independence (from Great Britain)

Declared our independence (from Great Britain)

Said that the United States is free (from Great Britain)

8. Kush ishte qellimi I Deklarates se Pavaresise?

Shpalli pavaresine tone (ndaj Britanise se Madhe)

Deklaroi pavaresine tone (ndaj Britanise se Madhe)

Tha se Shtetet e Bashkuara jane te lira (ndaj Britanise se Madhe)

9. What are two rights in the Declaration of Independence?

Life

Liberty

Pursuit of Happiness

9. Emerto dy te drejta te perfshira ne Deklaraten e Pavaresise.

E drejta per te jetuar

E drejta per liri

Ndjekja e lumturise

10. What is freedom of religion?

You can practice any religion, or not practice a religion.

10. C'fare do te thote liri feje?

E drejta per praktikim ose jo te cilesdo feje.

Ekonomi kapitaliste

Ekonomi tregu

11. What is the economic system in the United States?*

   capitalist economy

   market economy

11. Cili eshte sistemi ekonomik I Shteteve te Bashkuara?

   Ekonomi kapitaliste

   Ekonomi tregu

12. What is the "rule of law"?

   Everyone must follow the law

   Leaders must obey the law.

   Government must obey the law.

   No one is above the law

12. C'fare eshte "rregulli ligjor"?

   Te gjithe duhet te ndjekin ligjin

   Udheheqesit duhet ti binden ligjit

   Qeveria duhet ti bindet ligjit

   Askush nuk qendron mbi ligjin

System of Government

Sistemi Qeverises

13. Name one branch or part of the government.*

Congress

Legislative

President

Executive

The courts

Judicial

13. Emertoni nje dege ose pjese te qeverise.*

Kongresi

Dega legjislative

Presidenti

Dega ekzekutive

Gjykatat

Dega juridike

14. What stops one branch of government from becoming too powerful?

Checks and balances

Separation of powers

14. C'fare e parandalon nje dege qeveritare ndaj nje fuqizimi te tepert?

Kontroll dhe barazpeshe

Ndarje fuqishe

15. Who is in charge of the executive branch?

The President

15. Kush e drejton degen ekzekutive?

Presidenti

16. Who makes federal laws?

Congress

Senate and House (of Representatives)

(U.S. or national) legislature

16. Kush krijon ligje federale?

Kongresi

Senati dhe Perfaqesuesit Ligjor

Legjislatura (Amerikane ose kombetare)

17. What are the two parts of the U.S. Congress?*

The Senate and House (of Representatives)

17. Emerto dy pjese perberese te Kongresit Amerikan.*

Senati dhe Perfaqesuesit Ligjor

18. How many U.S. Senators are there?

One hundred (100)

18. Sa Senatore Amerikan jane ne teresi?

Njeqind (100)

19. We elect a U.S. Senator for how many years?

Six (6)

19. Per sa vite e zgjedhim nje Senator Amerikan?

Gjeshte (6)

20. Who is one of your state's U.S. Senators?*

See list below. Answers will vary. For District of Columbia

residents and residents of U.S. territories, the answer is

that D.C. (or the territory where the applicant lives) has no

U.S. Senators.

20. Kush eshte nje nga Senatoret Amerikan ne fuqi te shtetit tuaj?*

Pergjigjet jane te ndryshme.

See back of the book and write your answer here:

---

* If you are 65 years old or older and have been a legal permanent resident of the United States for 20 or more years, you may study just the questions that have been marked with an asterisk.

* Nese jeni 65 vjec e siper dhe keni qene banues I perhershem dhe I ligjshem I Shteteve te Bashkuara per 20 vite ose me shume, mund te mesoni vetem pyetjet te cilave I eshte bashkangjitur nje yll ne fund.

21. The House of Representatives has how many voting members?

Four hundred thirty-five (435)

21. Sa pjesetar permban Kongresi?

Katerqind e tridhjete e pese (435)

Dy (2)

22. We elect a U.S. Representative for how many years?

Two (2)

22. Per sa vite zgjidhet nje deputet Amerikan?

Dy (2)

23. Name your U.S. Representative.

Answers will vary. [Residents of territories with nonvoting

Delegates or resident Commissioners may provide the

name of that Delegate or Commissioner. Also acceptable

is any statement that the territory has no (voting)

Representatives in Congress.]

23. Emertoni deputetin e rrethit tuaj.

Pergjigjet jane te ndryshme

See back of the book and write your answer here:

____

24. Who does a U.S. Senator represent?

All people of the state

24. Ke perfaqeson Senatori Amerikan?

Te gjithe njerezit e shtetit.

25. Why do some states have more Representatives than other states?

There are three correct answers. You need to know one answer.

Because of the state's population

Because they have more people

Because some states have more people

25. Pse disa shtete kane me shume deputete se disa shtete te tjere?

Nga ndryshimi I popullsise

26. We elect a President for how many years?

Four (4)

26. Per sa vite e zgjedhim nje President?

Kater (4)

27. In what month do we vote for President?*

November

27. Ne cilin muaj behen votimet Presidencjale?

Nentor

28. What is the name of the President of the United States now?*.

Joe Biden

28. Si quhet presidenti I tanishem I Shteteve te Bashkuara?

Joe Biden

29. What is the name of the Vice President of the United States now?

Kamala Harris

29. Si quhet zevendes presidenti I tanishem I Shteteve te Bashkuara?

Kamala Harris

30. If the President can no longer serve, who becomes President?

The Vice President

30. Nese Presidenti nuk mund ti sherbeje me shtetit, kush behet President?

Zevendes Presidenti

31. If both the President and the Vice President can no longer serve, who becomes President?

The Speaker of the House

31. Nese Presidenti dhe Zevendes Presidenti nuk mund ti sherbejne me shtetit, kush behet President?

Kryetari I Kongresit

32. Who is the Commander in Chief of the military?

The President

32. Kush eshte Shefi Komandant I ushtrise?

Presidenti

33. Who signs bills to become laws?

The President

33. Kush firmos qe propozime ligjore te kthehen ne ligje?

Presidenti

34. Who vetoes bills?

The President

34. Kush mund ta refuzoje nje propozim ligjor?

Presidenti

35. What does the President's Cabinet do?

Advises the President

35. C'fare detyre ka Keshilli Presidencja?

Te keshillojne Presidentin

36. What are two Cabinet-level positions?

Secretary of Agriculture

Secretary of Commerce

Secretary of Defense

Secretary of Education

Secretary of Energy

Secretary of Housing and Urban Development

Secretary of the Interior

Secretary of State

Secretary of Transportation

Vice President

36. Emerto dy pozita te Keshillit Presidencjal.

Sekretari I agrikultures

Sekretari I tregetise

Sekretari I mbrojtjes

Sekretari I arsimit

Sekretari I energjitikes

Sekretari I strehimit dhe zhvillimit urbanistik

Sekretari I brendshem

Sekretari I shtetit

Sekretari I transportit

Zevendes Presidenti

37. What does the judicial branch do?

Reviews laws

Explains laws

Resolves disputes (disagreements)

Decides if a law goes against the Constitution

37. Kush eshte detyra e deges juridike?

Rishikon ligjet

shpjegon ligjet

Zgjidh mosmarreveshja

Vendos nese nje ligj eshte ne kundershtim me Kushtetuten

38. What is the highest court in the United States?

The Supreme Court

38. Kush eshte gjykata me e larte ne Shtetet e Bashkuara?

Gjykata supreme/e larte

39. How many justices are on the Supreme Court?

Nine (9)

39. Sa gjyqtar permban gjykata e larte?

Nente (9)

40. Who is the Chief Justice of the United States?

John G. Roberts, Jr.

40. Kush eshte gjyqtari me I larte I Shteteve te Bashkuara ne fuqi?

John Roberts

41. Under our Constitution, some powers belong to the federal government. What is one power of the federal government?

Know one of the following:

To print money

To declare war

To create an army

To make treaties

41. Sipak Kushtetutes Amerikane, disa fuqi I perkasin qeverise federale. Emerto nje fuqi te qeverise federale.

Te printoje leke

Te deklaroje lufte

Te krijoje nje ushtri

Te beje traktate

42. Under our Constitution, some powers belong to the states.

What is one power of the states?

Provide schooling and education

42. Sipak Kushtetutes Amerikane, disa fuqi I perkasin shteteve.

Emerto nje fuqi te shteteve.

Te parashohe shkollim dhe edukim

Te parashohe mbrojte (polici)

Te parashohe siguri (dege zjarrfikese)

Te te pajisi me patente automobilistike

Te miratoje marrjen dhe perdorimin e tokes

43. Who is the Governor of your state?

Answers will vary. Residents of the District of Columbia

and U.S. territories without a Governor should say "we

don't have a Governor."

43. Kush eshte Guvernatori ne fuqi I shtetit tuaj?

    Pergjigjet jane te ndryshme.

See back of the book and write your answer here:

---

44. What is the capital of your state?*

    Answers will vary. District of Columbia residents should

    answer that D.C. is not a state and does not have a

    capital. Residents of U.S. territories should name the

    capital of the territory.

44. Kush eshte kryeqyteti I shteti tuaj?

    Pergjigjet jane te ndryshme

See back of the book and write your answer here:

---

45. What are the two major political parties in the United States?*

    Democratic and Republican

45. Cilat jane dy partite me kryesore te Shteteve te Bashkuara?

    Partia Demokratike dhe ajo Republikane?*

46. What is the political party of the President now?

Democratic Party

46. Ciles parti politike I perket Presidenti ne fuqi?

Partia Demokratike

47. What is the name of the Speaker of the House of

Representatives now?

Kevin McCarthy

47. Si quhet Kryetari ne fuqi I Kongresit?

Kevin McCarthy

Rights and Responsibilities

Te drejtat dhe Pergjegjesite

48. There are four amendments to the Constitution about who can

vote. Describe one of them.

Citizens eighteen (18) and older can vote.

Any citizen can vote. (Women and men can vote.)

48. Kushtetuta permban kater amendamente per votuesit. Emerto

njeren prej tyre.

Shtetasit mbi moshen 18 vjecare mund te votojne

Votimi eshte falas

C'do qytetar shtetas mund te votoje (femra dhe meshkuj)

Shtetas meshkuj te cilesdo rrace mund te votojne

49. What is one responsibility that is only for United States citizens?*

Serve on a jury

Vote in a Federal election

49. Emerto nje pergjegjesi qe I perket vetem shtetaseve Amerikan.

Te sherbeje ne juri gjyqesore

Te votoje ne zgjedhje federale

50. What are two rights only for United States citizens?

Apply for a federal job

vote

50. Emerto nje te drejte qe I perket vetem shtetaseve Amerikan.

Te sherbejne ne juri gjyqesore

Votim

51. What are two rights of everyone living in the United States?

Freedom of speech

Freedom of assembly

Freedom to petition the government

Freedom of religious

The right to bear arms

51. Emerto dy te drejta te te gjithe banoreve te Amerikes.

Liri shprehje

Liri mbledhje

Liri per peticion ndaj qeverise

Liri te praktikimit fetar

E drejta per arme-mbajtje

52. What do we show loyalty to when we say the Pledge of Allegiance?

The United States and the flag

52. Ndaj kujt tregojme besnikeri kur betohemi?

Ndaj Shteteve te Bashkuara

Ndaj flamurit

53. What is one promise you make when you become a United States citizen?

Defend the Constitution and laws of the United States

53. Emerto nje premtim qe duhet te mbash kur behesh shtetas.

Mbro Kushtetuten dhe ligjet e Shteteve te Bashkuara

54. How old do citizens have to be to vote?*

Eighteen (18) and older

54. Sa vjec duhet te jene shtetasit Amerikane ne menyre qe te votojne per President?

Tetembedhjete (18)

55. What are two ways that Americans can participate in their democracy?

Vote

Join a political party

55. Emerto dy menyra qe percaktojne pjesemarrje demokratike te shtetaseve Amerikan.

Votim

Pjesemarrje ne parti politike

56. When is the last day you can send in federal income tax forms?*

April 15

56. Kur eshte dita e fundit qe mund te nisesh formularet e taksave federale?

15 Prill

57. When must all men register for the Selective Service?

Between eighteen (18) and twenty-six (26)

57. Kur duhet te gjithe meshkujt te regjistrohen per sherbime shteterore?

Ndermjet moshes tetembedhjete (18) dhe njezet e gjashte (26)

AMERICAN HISTORY

Historia Amerikane

Colonial Period and Independence

Periudha Koloniale dhe Pavaresia

58. What is one reason colonists came to America?

Freedom

Political liberty

58. Emerto nje arsye pse kolonistet erdhen ne Amerike?

Liri

Liri politike

59. Who lived in America before the Europeans arrived?

Native Americans

American Indians

59. Kush ka banuar ne Amerike perpara ardhjes se Europianeve?

Indjanet Amerikan

Amerikanet vendas

60. What group of people was taken to America and sold as slaves?

Africans

60. Cili grup njerezish jane sjelle ne Amerike dhe jane shitur si skllever?

Afrikanet

61. Why did the colonists fight the British?

Because of high taxes (taxation without representation)

Because the British army stayed in their houses (boarding, quartering)

Because they didn't have self-government

61. Pse luftuan kolonistet Britaniket?

Si rrjedhoje e taksave te larta

Sepse ushtaret Britanike ndejten ne shtepite e tyre

Sepse nuk kishin sistem vete-qeverises

62. Who wrote the Declaration of Independence?

Thomas Jefferson

62. Kush e shkroi Deklaraten e Pavaresise?

Thomas Jefferson

63. When was the Declaration of Independence adopted?

July 4, 1776

63. Kur u adoptua Deklarata e Pavaresise?

4 Korrik, 1776

64. There were 13 original states. Name three.

New Hampshire

Massachusetts

Rhode IslandConnecticut

New York

New Jersey

Pennsylvania

Delaware

Maryland

Virginia

North Carolina

South Carolina

Georgia

64. Fillimisht kane qene 13 shtete origjinale. Emerto tre.

New Hampshire

Massachusetts

Rhode IslandConnecticut

New York

New Jersey

Pennsylvania

Delaware

Maryland

Virginia

North Carolina

South Carolina

Georgia

65. What happened at the Constitutional Convention?

The Constitution was written.

65. C'fare ndodhi ne Kuvendin Kushtetues?

U shkrua Kushtetuta

66. When was the Constitution written?

1787

66. Kur u shkrua Kushtetuta?

1787

67. The Federalist Papers supported the passage of the U.S.

Constitution. Name one of the writers.

James Madison

Alexander Hamilton

John Jay

67. Dokumentat Federaliste mbeshteten kalimin e Kushtetutes

Amerikane. Emerto nje nga shkrimtaret.

James Madison

Alexander Hamilton

John Jay

68. What is one thing Benjamin Franklin is famous for?

U.S. diplomat

68. Emerto nje nga gjerat per te cilat Benjamin Franklin eshte I

njohur.

Diplomat Amerikan

69. Who is the "Father of Our Country"?

George Washington

69. Kush është "Ati ynë i Vendit"?

George Washington

70. Who was the first President?*

George Washington

70. Kush ishte Presidenti I pare?

George Washington

71. What territory did the United States buy from France in 1803?

The Louisiana Territory

71. Cilin territor bleu Amerika nga Franca ne 1803?

The Louisiana Territory

72. Name one war fought by the United States in the 1800s..

Spanish-American War

72. Emerto nje beteje te luftuar nga Shtetet e Bashkuara ne vitet 1800.

Lufta Amerikano-Spanjolle

73. Name the U.S. war between the North and the South.

The Civil War

73. Emerto luften Amerikane ndermjet Veriut dhe Jugut.

Lufta civile

74. Name one problem that led to the Civil War.

Slavery

Economics

State Rights

74. Emerto nje problem qe shkaktoi Luften Civile.

Skllaveria

Shkaqe ekonomike

E drejta e shteteve

75. What was one important thing that Abraham Lincoln did?*

Freed the slaves (Emancipation Proclamation)

75. Emerto nje arritje te rendesishme qe ka kryer Ibrahim Linkolni.

Liruar robërit (Emancipimi Shpallja)

76. What did the Emancipation Proclamation do?

Freed the slaves

76. C'fare roli pati Shpallja e Emancipimit?

Liruar robërit (Emancipimi Shpallja)

77. What did Susan B. Anthony do?

Fought for women's rights

77. Per se njihet Susan B. Anthony?

Luftoi per te drejtat e grave

Recent American History
and Other Important Historical Information

Historia bashkekohore dhe informacjone historike te tjera te rendesishme

78. Name one war fought by the United States in the 1900s.*

World War I

World War II

78. Emerto nje beteje te luftuar nga Shtetet e Bashkuara.

Lufta e Pare boterore

Lufta e Dyte boterore

79. Who was President during World War I?

Woodrow Wilson

79. Kush ishte President gjate Luftes se Pare boterore?

Woodrow Wilson

80. Who was President during the Great Depression and World War II?

Franklin Roosevelt

80. Kush ishte President gjate Depresjonit te Madh dhe Luftes se Dyte boterore?

Franklin Roosevelt

81. Who did the United States fight in World War II?

Japan, Germany and Italy

81. Kundra kujt luftoi Amerika gjate Luftes se Dyte botere?

Japonine, Gjermanine, dhe Italine

82. Before he was President, Eisenhower was a general. What war was he in?

World War II

82. Perpara se te behej President, Ajzenhauer ishte gjeneral. Ne cilen lufte ishte pjesemarres?

Lufta e Dyte boterore

83. During the Cold War, what was the main concern of the United States?.

Communism

83. Kush ishte shqetesimi kryesor I Amerikes gjate Luftes se Ftohte?

Komunizmi.

84. What movement tried to end racial discrimination?

civil rights movement

84. Cila levizje tentoi ti jepte fund dallimit rracjal?

Levizja per te drejtat civile

85. What did Martin Luther King, Jr. do?*

Fought for civil rights

85. Per se njihet Martin Luther Kingu I dyte?

Luftoi per te drejta civile

86. What major event happened on September 11, 2001 in the United States?

Terrorists attacked the United States..

86. C'fare ngjarje madhore ndodhi me 11 Shtator, 2001, ne Shtetet e Bashkuara?

Terroristet sulmuan Shtetet e Bashkuara

87. Name one American Indian tribe in the United States.

Cherokee

Navajo

87. Emerto nje fis Indian-Amerikan te Shteteve te Bashkuara.

Cherokee

Navajo

Apache

[Adjudicators will be supplied with a complete list.]

INTEGRATED CIVICS

Qytetarim I Integruar

Geography / Gjeografi

88. Name one of the two longest rivers in the United States.

   Missouri or Mississippi river

88. Emerto nje nga dy liqenet me te gjate te Shteteve te

Bashkuar.

   Missouri ose Mississippi lumë

89. What ocean is on the West Coast of the United States?

   Pacific Ocean

89. Cili oqean lag bregun Perendimor te Amerikes?

   Oqeani Pacifik

90. What ocean is on the East Coast of the United States?

   Atlantic Ocean

90. Cili oqean lag bregun Lindor te Amerikes?

   Oqeani Atlantik

91. Name one U.S. territory.

US Virgin Islands

American Samoa

Mariana Islands

Guam

91. Emerto nje territor te Amerikes.Porto Riko

Ishujt e Virgjer Amerikan

Samoa Amerikane

Ishujt Verjor Marjana

Guama

92. Name one state that borders Canada.

Maine

New Hampshire

Vermont

New York

Pennsylvania

Ohio

Michigan

Minnesota

North Dakota

Montana

Idaho

Washington

Alaska

92. Emerto nje shtet ne kufi te Kanadase.

Maine

New Hampshire

Vermont

New York

Pennsylvania

Ohio

Michigan

Minnesota

North Dakota

Montana

Idaho

Washington

Alaska

93. Name one state that borders Mexico.

California

Arizona

New Mexico

Texas

93. Emerto nje shtet ne kufi te Meksikes.

Kalifornia

Arizona

Meksika e Re

Teksas

94. What is the capital of the United States?*

Washington, D.C.

94. Kush eshte kryeqyteti I Shteteve te bashkuara?

Uashingtoni, D.C.

95. Where is the Statue of Liberty?*

New York Harbor

Liberty Island

[Also acceptable are New Jersey, New York, and the

Hudson River.]

95. Ku ndodhet Statuja e Lirise?

Në Nju Jork

Liberty Island

[Gjithashtu pranueshme janë të New Jersey, New York,

dhe në lumin Hudson.]

Symbols / Simbolet

96. Why does the flag have 13 stripes?

Because there were 13 original colonies

96. Pse ka flamuri 13 vija?

Sepse fillimisht ishin 13 koloni (shtete) origjinale

Sepse vijat perfaqesojne kolonite (shtetet) origjinale

97. Why does the flag have 50 stars?*

Because there is one star for each state

97. Pse ka 50 yje flamuri?

Sepse nuk është një yll për secilin shtet

Sepse secili yll perfaqeson nje shtet

Sepse jane 50 shtete

98. What is the name of the national anthem?

The Star-Spangled Banner

98. Si quhet Himni I Flamurit?

Star -Spangled Banner

Holidays / Festat.

99. When do we celebrate Independence Day?*

July 4

99. Kur e festojme Diten e Pavaresise?

Me 4 Korrik

100. Name two national U.S. holidays.

Martin Luther King Day

President's Day

Independence Day

Workers Day

Columbus Day

Veterans Day

Thanksgiving Day

Christmas

100. Emerto dy festa Amerikane kombetare.

Dita e Martin Luther Kingut

Dita e Presidentit

Dita e Pavaresise

Dita e Punetoreve

Dita e Kolumbusit

Dita e Veteraneve

Dita e Falenderimeve

Krishtlindja

SAMPLE WRITTEN SENTENCES

You will be asked to write a sample sentence. Normally you can make up to three (3) errors in writing and still pass the test.

Be careful to listen to each word the examiner reads. Make sure to write each word, even if you think it is not needed grammatically, if the examiner reads a word; please write out every word that is dictated.

1) A senator is elected for 6 years.

2) Michael Pence is the Vice President of the United States.

3) All people want to be free.

4) America is the land of freedom.

5) All American citizens have the right to vote.

6) America is the home of the brave.

7) America is the land of the free.

8) Donald J Trump is the President of the United States.

9) Citizens have the right to vote.

10) Congress is part of the American government.

11) Congress meets in Washington DC.

12) Congress passes laws in the United States.

13) George Washington was the first president.

14) I want to be a citizen of the United States.

15) I want to be an American citizen.

16) I want to become an American so I can vote.

17) It is important for all citizens to vote.

18) Many people come to America for freedom.

19) Many people have died for freedom.

20) Martha Washington was the first lady.

21) Only Congress can declare war.

22) Our Government is divided into three branches.

23) People in America have the right to freedom.

24) People vote for the President in November.

25) The American flag has stars and stripes.

26) The American flag has 13 stripes.

27) The capital of the United States is Washington DC.

28) The colors of the flag are red white and blue.

29) The Constitution is the supreme law of our land.

30) The flag of the United States has 50 stars.

31) The House and Senate are parts of Congress

32) The President enforces the laws.

33) The President has the power of veto.

34) The President is elected every 4 years.

35) The President lives in the White House.

36) The President lives in Washington D.C.

37) The President must be an American citizen.

38) The President must be born in the United States.

39) The President signs bills into law.

40) The stars of the American flag are white.

41) The White House is in Washington, DC.

42) The United States flag is red white and blue.

43) The United States of America has 50 states.

Members of the Senate
Senators of the 118th Congress

Representatives are subject to change.

Find your state to identify your two Senators

Source: http://Senate.gov Updated January 2023

What is a class? - Article I, section 3 of the Constitution requires the Senate to be divided into three classes for purposes of elections. Senators are elected to six-year terms, and every two years the members of one class—approximately one-third of the senators—face election or reelection. Terms for senators in Class I expire in 2019, Class II in 2021, and Class III in 2023.

U.S. State Postal Abbreviations List

Alabama – AL   Alaska – AK   Arizona – AZ   Arkansas - AR

California – CA   Colorado – CO   Connecticut - CT

Delaware – DE   District of Columbia - DC

Florida - FL

Georgia - GA

Hawaii - HI

Idaho – ID   Illinois – IL   Indiana – IN   Iowa - IA

Kansas – KS   Kentucky - KY

Louisiana - LA

Maine – ME   Maryland – MD   Massachusetts – MA
Michigan – MI   Minnesota – MN   Mississippi – MS
Missouri – MO   Montana - MT

Nebraska – NE   Nevada – NV   New Hampshire – NH

New Jersey – NJ   New Mexico – NM   New York – NY
North Carolina – NC   North Dakota - ND

Ohio – OH   Oklahoma – OK   Oregon - OR

Pennsylvania - PA

Rhode Island - RI

South Carolina – SC   South Dakota - SD

Tennessee – TN   Texas - TX

Utah - UT

Vermont – VT   Virginia - VA

Washington – WA   West Virginia – WV   Wisconsin – WI
Wyoming - WY

US Commonwealth and Territories

American Samoa – AS   Federated States of Micronesia – FM
Guam – GU   Marshall Islands - MH

Northern Mariana Islands – MP   Palau – PW   Puerto Rico –
PR   Virgin Islands

Senators of the 118th Congress

Tommy Tuberville	Republican	Alabama
Katie Britt	Republican	Alabama
Lisa Murkowski	Republican	Alaska
Dan Sullivan	Republican	Alaska
Kyrsten Sinema	Democratic	Arizona
Mark Kelly	Democratic	Arizona
John Boozman	Republican	Arkansas
Tom Cotton	Republican	Arkansas
Dianne Feinstein	Democratic	California
Alex Padilla	Democratic	California

Michael Bennet	Democratic	Colorado
John Hickenlooper	Democratic	Colorado
Richard Blumenthal	Democratic	Connecticut
Chris Murphy	Democratic	Connecticut
Tom Carper	Democratic	Delaware
Chris Coons	Democratic	Delaware
Marco Rubio	Republican	Florida
Rick Scott	Republican	Florida
Jon Ossoff	Democratic	Georgia
Brian Schatz	Democratic	Hawaii
Mazie Hirono	Democratic	Hawaii
Mike Crapo	Republican	Idaho
Jim Risch	Republican	Idaho
Dick Durbin	Democratic	Illinois
Tammy Duckworth	Democratic	Illinois
Todd Young	Republican	Indiana
Mike Braun	Republican	Indiana
Chuck Grassley	Republican	Iowa
Joni Ernst	Republican	Iowa
Jerry Moran	Republican	Kansas
Roger Marshall	Republican	Kansas
Mitch McConnell	Republican	Kentucky
Rand Paul	Republican	Kentucky
Bill Cassidy	Republican	Louisiana
John Neely Kennedy	Republican	Louisiana
Susan Collins	Republican	Maine
Angus King	Independent	Maine
Ben Cardin	Democratic	Maryland
Chris Van Hollen	Democratic	Maryland
Elizabeth Warren	Democratic	Massachusetts
Ed Markey	Democratic	Massachusetts
Debbie Stabenow	Democratic	Michigan
Gary Peters	Democratic	Michigan
Amy Klobuchar	Democratic	Minnesota
Tina Smith	Democratic	Minnesota

Roger Wicker	Republican	Mississippi
Cindy Hyde-Smith	Republican	Mississippi
Josh Hawley	Republican	Missouri
Eric Schmitt	Republican	Missouri
Jon Tester	Democratic	Montana
Steve Daines	Republican	Montana
Deb Fischer	Republican	Nebraska
Ben Sasse	Republican	Nebraska
TBD	Republican	Nebraska
Catherine Cortez Masto	Democratic	Nevada
Jacky Rosen	Democratic	Nevada
Jeanne Shaheen	Democratic	New Hampshire
Maggie Hassan	Democratic	New Hampshire
Bob Menendez	Democratic	New Jersey
Cory Booker	Democratic	New Jersey
Martin Heinrich	Democratic	New Mexico
Ben Ray Luján	Democratic	New Mexico
Chuck Schumer	Democratic	New York
Kirsten Gillibrand	Democratic	New York
Thom Tillis	Republican	North Carolina
Ted Budd *	Republican	North Carolina
John Hoeven	Republican	North Dakota
Kevin Cramer	Republican	North Dakota
Sherrod Brown	Democratic	Ohio
J. D. Vance *	Republican	Ohio
James Lankford	Republican	Oklahoma
Markwayne Mullin *	Republican	Oklahoma
Ron Wyden	Democratic	Oregon
Jeff Merkley	Democratic	Oregon
Bob Casey, Jr.	Democratic	Pennsylvania
John Fetterman	Democratic	Pennsylvania
Jack Reed	Democratic	Rhode Island
Sheldon Whitehouse	Democratic	Rhode Island

Lindsey Graham	Republican	South Carolina
Tim Scott	Republican	South Carolina
John Thune	Republican	South Dakota
Mike Rounds	Republican	South Dakota
Marsha Blackburn	Republican	Tennessee
Bill Hagerty	Republican	Tennessee
John Cornyn	Republican	Texas
Ted Cruz	Republican	Texas
Mike Lee	Republican	Utah
Mitt Romney	Republican	Utah
Bernie Sanders	Independent	Vermont
Peter Welch	Democratic	Vermont
Mark Warner	Democratic	Virginia
Tim Kaine	Democratic	Virginia
Patty Murray	Democratic	Washington
Maria Cantwell	Democratic	Washington
Joe Manchin	Democratic	West Virginia
Shelley Moore Capito	Republican	West Virginia
Ron Johnson	Republican	Wisconsin
Tammy Baldwin	Democratic	Wisconsin
John Barrasso	Republican	Wyoming
Cynthia Lummis	Republican	Wyoming

List of State Governors

Governors are subject to change. District of Columbia residents should answer that D.C. is not a state and does not have a capital. Residents of U.S. territories should name the capital of the territory.
Governors are subject to change. District of Columbia residents should answer that D.C. is not a state and does not have a capital. Residents of U.S. territories should name the capital of the territory.

Source: https://www.nga.org/governors/

*Denotes newly elected Governors

Alabama – Kay Ivey

Alaska – Mike Dunaway

Arizona – To be determined

Arkansas – Asa Hutchinson.

California – Gavin Newsom

Colorado – Jared Polis

Connecticut – Ned Lamont

Delaware – John Carney

Florida – Ron DeSantis

Georgia – Brian Kemp

Hawaii – David Ige

Idaho – Brad Little

Illinois – J.B. Pritzker

Indiana – Eric Holcomb

Iowa – Kim Reynolds

Kansas – Laura Kelly

Kentucky – Andy Beshear

Louisiana – John Bel Edwards

Maine – Janet Mills

Maryland – Larry Hogan

Massachusetts – Charlie Baker

Michigan – Gretchen Whitmer

Minnesota – Tim Walz

Mississippi – Tate Reeves

Missouri – Mike Parson

Montana – Greg Gianforte*

Nebraska – Jim Pillen

Nevada – Steve Sisolak

New Hampshire – Chris Sununu

New Jersey – Phil Murphy

New Mexico – Michelle Lujan Grisham

New York – Kathy Hochul

North Carolina – Ray Cooper

North Dakota – Doug Burgum

Ohio – Mike DeWine

Oklahoma – Kevin Stitt

Oregon – Tina Kotek

Pennsylvania – Josh Shapiro

Rhode Island – Daniel McKee

South Carolina – Henri McMaster

South Dakota – Kristi Noem

Tennessee – Bill Lee

Texas – Greg Abbott

Utah – Spencer Cox

Vermont – Phil Scott

Virginia – Glenn Youngkin

Washington – Jay Inslee

West Virginia – Jim Justice

Wisconsin – Tony Evers

Wyoming – Mark Gordon

Avoid Scams

From the USCIS website: http://www.uscis.gov/avoidscams
The wrong help can hurt
Are you getting the right immigration help?
Many people offer help with immigration services. Unfortunately, not all are authorized to do so. While many of these unauthorized practitioners mean well, all too many of them are out to rip you off. This is against the law and may be considered an immigration services scam.
If you need help filing an application or petition with USCIS, be sure to seek assistance from the right place, and from people that are authorized to help. Going to the wrong place can:
Delay your application or petition
Cost you unnecessary fees
Possibly lead to removal proceedings
This site can help you avoid immigration services scams. Remember: Know the facts when it comes to immigration assistance, because the Wrong Help Can Hurt.
Tools to Help You Avoid Scammers
USCIS wants to combat immigration services scams by equipping applicants, legal service providers and community-based organizations with the knowledge and tools they need to detect and protect themselves from dishonest practices.
To accomplish this goal, USCIS launched the Unauthorized Practice of Immigration Law (UPIL) Initiative. As part of the effort, we've partnered with several government agencies to identify resources that can help you avoid immigration services scams.
Empower yourself by using our online educational resources, which include:
The top things to know before and after filing an application or petition
A list of common immigration services scams
State-by-state information on where you can report an immigration services scam
Advice on finding authorized legal help
Information on becoming an authorized legal immigration service provider
Educational tools you can print and share
This page can be found at: http://www.uscis.gov/avoidscams.

ABOUT THE AUTHOR

Mike Swedenberg saw a need to assemble a study guide to help those persons wishing to immigrate to the United States whose second language is English. This study guide is annotated with the names of current Representatives that all applicants must know. The list is current for State Governors, US Senators and US Congressmen. This list will be updated at each election cycle.

Other books by the Author
The Road Warrior a sales manual
Advertising Copywriting and the Unique Selling Proposition
Smart Money Stupid Money
21 ½ Things to Know Before Self-Publishing
How to Publish an eBook